*Unibroue ales work wonders in the kitchen. However, recipes made with beer wouldn't exist if it weren't for beer recipes.*

*Beer being historically the first alcoholic beverage resulting from a cooking process, I enjoy brewing as well as cooking, and above all cooking with beer.*

*In the brewhouse, as in the kitchen, the secret of success lies in balancing multiple flavors. That's why I pay such close attention to the choice and dosage of ingredients when I create Unibroue ales—so you can enjoy a perfectly balanced and flavorful product.*

*With their spicy, fruity notes and complex aromas, our ales lend a special touch to gourmet dishes, marinades, sauces, cocktails, and even desserts. Discover the magic of cooking with beer with the great recipe ideas in this book. It's perfect for beer lovers—and anyone who appreciates fine cuisine.*

*Unibroue ales are foods in their own right! Give them a seat at your table!*

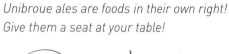

**Jerry Vietz**
*Brewmaster*

# THE UNIBROUE EXPERIENCE

## We aim to wake all your senses!

*YOU ARE HOLDING A SELECTION OF THE BEST RECIPES INSPIRED BY OUR BEERS.
ENJOY!*

*Since 1990, Unibroue has become one of the best breweries in the world, drawing inspiration from the great brewing traditions developed in Europe, particularly in Belgium. Food lovers will discover dishes that pair perfectly well with delicious craft beers. Unibroue is not only sharing recipes but also special moments by reaching out to the community! Our new Unibroue "Bière et Bouffe" food truck was built to spoil our biggest fans during gatherings and events. Unibroue loves to meet you and even plans contests to do so in your own home.*

*You can integrate our beers in your everyday cooking in several ways. Whether you are looking for a delicious marinade or a perfectly balanced sauce, you will find it in this book. Or you crave classic comfort food or an original recipe? Whether you wish to cool down or warm up, you will be charmed!*

# TABLE OF CONTENTS

**BEER AND SPICES** ....... 6

**MARINADES, GRAVYS AND PRESERVES** ....... 9

Beer and lime marinade for shrimp and fish ....... 11
Beer marinade and herb butter for pork tenderloin ....... 12
Marinade for skirt steak ....... 13
Marinade for spicy chicken drumsticks ....... 13
BBQ sauce with Maudite ....... 14
Steak sauce with Noire de Chambly ....... 16
Creamy Blanche de Chambly sauce ....... 16
Hot pepper sauce ....... 17
Sauce for beef bourguignon with La Fin du Monde ....... 17
Homemade marmalade with Blanche de Chambly ....... 19
Caramelized onions with Maudite ....... 20
Marinated Jalapeños with À Tout le Monde ....... 21
Rhubarb jam with Éphémère Apple ....... 21

**FOOD TRUCK DISHES** ....... 23

Asian buns ....... 25
Salmon tartare ....... 26
Braised beef sandwich ....... 29
Shrimp vermicelli ....... 30
Chicken satay with mango and pink peppercorns ....... 32
Spare ribs with Maudite ....... 35
Fried pickles with Raftman ....... 36
Panacotta with Éphémère Blueberry ....... 39
Poor man's pudding with Maudite ....... 41

**ON THE ROAD** ....... 43

Panko crabcake ....... 45
Modern-day grilled cheese ....... 47
Coleslaw with Raftman ....... 48
Pulled beef poutine ....... 51

**COOKING WITH UNIBROUE** ....... 53

Cod fillets with Trois Pistoles ....... 54
Bread with beer and garlic flowers ....... 57
Bacon jam ....... 59
Pork meatballs ....... 61

**FAVORITES AND CLASSICS** ....... 65

Cheesy dip with beer caramelized onions ....... 66
Grilled beef back steak ....... 69
Rustic pizza with marinated chicken ....... 70
Cheese fondue with Blonde de Chambly ....... 73
Typical Toulouse cassoulet ....... 74
Éphémère apple pie ....... 77
Chocolate Caramel Brownies à 17ᵉ Grande Réserve ....... 78

Index ....... 80
Credits ....... 83

### WHITE ALE
**5% ABV**
*Suggested serving temperature: 4°C (39°F) – 6°C (43°F)*
*Glass: Flute*

Citrus, coriander and clove aromas. Wheat, orange and spice notes. Nice balance sugar/acidity, honey-like finish. No bitterness.

coriander, cloves or rosemary, Madagascar black pepper

31 international medals

### SAISON ALE
**5% ABV**
*Suggested serving temperature: 4° (39°F) – 6°C (43°F)*
*Glass: Flute*

Smooth blond ale with a bouquet of lemongrass, wildflowers and hops. Sustained effervescence, crisp acidity followed by a sweet finish. Astringent finish.

lemony thyme, pink pepper, Camargue salt

10 international medals

### BLACK ALE (STRONG ALE)
**6.2% ABV**
*Suggested serving temperature: 6°C (43°F) – 8°C (47°F)*
*Glass: Flute or tulip*

Fruity nose with notes of roasted coffee beans and licorice. Smooth sweet flavors of roasted grains and spices with a chocolaty finish.

anise, fennel, Provencal herbs

9 international medals

### WHITE ALE BREWED WITH APPLES
**5,5% ABV**
*Suggested serving temperature: 6°C (43°F) – 8°C (47°F)*
*Glass: Tulip*

Attractive golden color, effervescent foam and mouth-watering bouquet of Granny smith apples and spices. Hint of sweetness, hint of tartness.

nutmeg, ginger, cinnamon or thyme and bay leaf

21 international medals

### WHITE ALE BREWED WITH BLUEBERRIES
**5.5% ABV**
*Suggested serving temperature: 6°C (43°F) – 8°C (47°F)*
*Glass: Tulip*

Wild berry aromas, citrus notes. Vivid blueberry flavor with a complementary refreshing acidity.

fresh thyme, lime, honey

### BELGIAN STYLE DRY HOPPED SAISON
**4.5% ABV**
*Suggested serving temperature: 4° (39°F) – 6°C (43°F)*
*Glass: Flute or tulip*

Delicately spiced, citrusy and slightly tart with hints of tropical fruit such as mango and lychee.

Juniper berry, basil, cardamom, lemongrass, cumin, tarragon, ginger, lime, mint, parsley, horseradish, sage, wasabi

1 international medal

# BEER AND SPICES

### SMOKED ALE
**5.5% ABV**
*Suggested serving temperature: 8°C (47°F) – 10°C (50°F)*
*Glass: Tulip or snifter*

Beautiful amber red colour and rich cream-coloured foam. Smoked aroma with subtle herb notes followed by rich flavours of malt, wood and spices.

cinnamon, cardamom, nutmeg, pumpkin

6 international medals

### DUBBEL ALE (STRONG ALE)
**8% ABV**
*Suggested serving temperature: 12°C (54°F) – 14°C (57°F)*
*Glass: Snifter*

Nose of caramel malt, oranges and spices, with coriander and clove notes. Smooth caramelized sugar taste, light roasting notes and spicy finish.

coriander, Thai peppers or paprika

29 international medals

### TRIPEL ALE (EXTRA STRONG ALE)
**9% ABV**
*Suggested serving temperature: 12°C (54°F) – 14°C (57°F)*
*Glass: Tulip*

Floral bouquet, aromas of spice, coriander, malt and alcohol. Surprisingly smooth with hints of cereal and white pepper, distinct alcohol taste.

mint, dried hibiscus flowers or pink pepper, vanilla bean or lemon thyme, mustard seeds

44 international medals

### WHITE ALE (EXTRA STRONG ALE)
**9% ABV**
*Suggested serving temperature: 8°C (47°F) – 10°C (50°F)*
*Glass: Tulip, snifter*

Aromas of vanilla and fruitcake, beeswax, flowers and honey.
Sweet, distinct alcohol taste with hints of bananas, hops and spices.

lemongrass, citrus, coriander, nutmeg

17 international medals

### QUADRUPEL ALE (EXTRA STRONG ALE)
**9% ABV**
*Suggested serving temperature: 8°C (47°F) – 10°C (50°F)*
*Glass: Chalice or snifter*

Strong malt nose, roasted aromas with brown rum and spices.
Full-bodied, ripe fruit, figs, prunes, lightly roasted grains.

ginger, Jamaican peppers or anise

30 international medals

GRANDE RÉSERVE 17
2016

### EXTRA STRONG DARK ALE
**10% ABV**
*Suggested serving temperature: 12°C (54°F) – 14°C (57°F)*
*Glass: Chalice or tulip*

Complex bouquet of roasted malt, hops and aromatic spice notes with vanilla undertones. Flavors are intensely malty, slightly sweet and hoppy with mocha & cocoa accents and a subtle oaky finish.

Vanilla bean, cocoa bean, smoked paprika

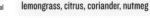

21 international medals

# MARINADES, SAUCES AND PRESERVES

◆

## – Beer is coming to your table –

Emphasize a scent, enhance a flavour, create an aroma?
Unibroue beers bring flavour to your kitchen. With their complex aromatics,
they become the perfect ingredient to add a variety of aromas
and flavours to your dishes.

Perfect for your friends
who don't eat gluten,
red meat or dairy... :)

# BEER AND LIME MARINADE FOR SHRIMP AND FISH

## INGREDIENTS

*FOR 500 ML (2 CUPS)*

- 125 ml (1/2 cup) Maudite or Blanche de Chambly beer (to taste, according to desired intensity)
- 350 ml (1 1/2 cups) French shallots, minced
- 125 ml (1/2 cup) fresh coriander, chopped
- 125 ml (1/2 cup) Thai peppers, chopped
- 60 ml (1/4 cup) garlic, minced
- 250 ml (1 cup) extra virgin olive oil
- 180 ml (3/4 cup) fresh lime juice
- 30 ml (2 tbsp) tequila
- 15 ml (1 tbsp) ground black pepper
- 5 ml (1 tsp) anise seeds
- 12 to 15 peeled raw shrimp

## DIRECTIONS

- Combine all the ingredients in a bowl and mix.
- Add shrimp to the mixture and marinate in the refrigerator for about 2 hours prior to grilling on the BBQ.

**RECIPE AND PAIRINGS**

COMBINE

MARINATE

GRILL

# BEER MARINADE AND HERB BUTTER FOR PORK TENDERLOIN

## INGREDIENTS

*FOR 175 ML (2/3 CUP)*

### Marinade

- 125 ml (1/2 cup) Blonde de Chambly or À Tout le Monde beer
- 2 whole shallots
- 1 garlic clove
- 15 ml (1 tbsp) pressed lemon juice
- 15 ml (1 tbsp) Dijon mustard
- 7 ml (1/2 tbsp) old-style mustard
- 5 ml (1 tsp) Jamaican peppers
- 15 ml (1 tbsp) fresh thyme
- 2 pork tenderloins
- Salt and fresh ground pepper to taste

### Herb butter

- 200 g (1/2 lb) softened butter
- 4 garlic cloves, finely chopped
- 15 ml (1 tbsp) fresh coriander, finely chopped
- 15 ml (1 tbsp) fresh chives, finely chopped
- 15 ml (1 tbsp) fresh parsley, finely chopped
- 5 ml (1 tsp) dried lemon thyme
- 45 ml (3 tbsp) fresh lemon juice
- Salt to taste

## DIRECTIONS

### MARINADE

- Chop the shallots and the garlic.
- Combine the shallots and garlic with the mustards, the lemon juice, the Jamaican peppers, the thyme, the Blonde de Chambly, salt and pepper and puree in a blender.
- Marinate the pork tenderloins in this marinade in the refrigerator for 4 to 8 hours for best results.

### HERB BUTTER

- Whip the butter in a warm salad bowl until foamy.
- Press the garlic and chop finely.
- Add garlic, fresh herbs, lemon juice and salt to the butter. Mix vigorously.
- Place butter on plastic wrap, roll the butter into a cylinder shape and harden in the refrigerator.
- Cut the butter into slices at serving time. Place a slice of herb butter on the steaming pork.

RECIPE AND PAIRINGS

*The perfect recipe to impress the in-laws with a French bistro style dinner.*

# MARINADE FOR SKIRT STEAK

### INGREDIENTS

*FOR 350 ML (1 1/2 CUPS)*

- 250 ml (1 cup) Trois Pistoles or Terrible beer
- 4 French shallots, minced
- 2 garlic cloves, finely chopped
- 15 ml (1 tbsp) honey
- 15 ml (1 tbsp) lemon zest
- 15 ml (1 tbsp) fresh ginger, chopped
- 30 ml (2 tbsp) sesame oil
- 30 ml (2 tbsp) maple syrup
- 30 ml (2 tbsp) brown sugar
- 4 skirt steaks
- Salt and Madagascar pepper

### DIRECTIONS

- In a saucepan, mix all the ingredients for the marinade.
- Bring to a boil, lower the heat and simmer for about 5 minutes.
- Remove the marinade from heat and cool.
- Place the beef in a large dish and coat with the marinade.
- Marinate the meat 4 to 6 hours in the refrigerator.

# MARINADE FOR SPICY CHICKEN DRUMSTICKS

### INGREDIENTS

*FOR 350 ML (1 1/2 CUPS)*

- 1 bottle of Raftman or Éphémère Apple beer (341ml / 12 oz)
- 15 ml (1 tbsp) coarse salt
- 1 x 1 inch piece fresh ginger, minced
- 1 star anise
- 2 cloves
- 5 ml (1 tsp) cinnamon
- 5 ml (1 tsp) nutmeg
- Madagascar pepper, to taste
- 12 chicken drumsticks with the skin (can be replaced by chicken breasts or brochettes)

### DIRECTIONS

- In a saucepan, at medium-high setting, heat one third of the Raftman bottle, with the coarse salt.
- Add the other ingredients.
- Mix vigorously and transfer in a large leak-proof plastic bag.
- Add the chicken and marinate in the refrigerator for 12 to 24 hours.

# BBQ SAUCE
# WITH MAUDITE

## INGREDIENTS

*FOR 500 ML (2 CUPS)*

- 125 ml (1/2 cup) Maudite beer
- 125 ml (1/2 cup) crushed tomato pulp
- 65 ml (1/4 cup) molasses
- 125 ml (1/2 cup) ketchup
- 1 red bell pepper, chopped
- 1 onion, finely chopped
- 1 Jalapeño pepper with the seeds, oven-roasted
- 2 garlic cloves
- 15 ml (1 tbsp) extra virgin olive oil
- 5 ml (1 tsp) corn starch
- 5 ml (1 tsp) mustard seeds
- 30 ml (2 tbsp) sugar
- Salt
- Pepper

## DIRECTIONS

- In a saucepan, heat the oil on medium-high heat. Cook the onion for 3 minutes, until soft.
- Add the garlic and the bell pepper and continue cooking for 5 minutes.
- Pour the beer and simmer until the liquid is reduced by half.
- Add the rest of the ingredients, except for the corn starch, and cook for about 10 minutes.
- Dilute starch slightly with water and add it to the recipe to thicken the sauce. Macerate for an additional 10 minutes.
- Remove from heat and cool.
- Blend in a food processor.

*NOTE: Warning: warm mixtures tend to "explode" in the mixer.*

**RECIPE**

**BEER PAIRINGS**

*Best ribs in town!* #1

# STEAK SAUCE WITH NOIRE DE CHAMBLY

## INGREDIENTS

*FOR 350 ML (1 1/2 CUPS)*

- 125 ml (1/2 cup) Noire de Chambly or Trois Pistoles beer
- 15 ml (1 tbsp) extra virgin olive oil
- 1 red onion, finely chopped
- 3 garlic cloves, finely chopped
- 30 ml (2 tbsp) maple syrup
- 30 ml (2 tbsp) white wine vinegar
- 125 ml (1/2 cup) tomato paste
- 125 ml (1/2 cup) water
- 75 ml (1/3 cup) oyster sauce (Hoisin)
- 5 ml (1 tsp) Sriracha sauce

## DIRECTIONS

- In a saucepan, heat the oil on medium-high heat. Cook the onions 3 minutes until tender.
- Add the garlic and simmer for one minute.
- Incorporate the beer and continue cooking.
- In a separate bowl, mix the tomato paste and the water.
- Add the mixture, syrup, vinegar, oyster sauce and Sriracha sauce.
- Cook for 20 minutes on medium-low heat, mixing occasionally until sauce becomes smooth and thickens.

# CREAMY BLANCHE DE CHAMBLY SAUCE

## INGREDIENTS

*FOR 500 ML (2 CUPS)*

- 250 ml (1 cup) Blanche de Chambly beer
- 200 ml (3/4 cup) 15% cooking cream
- 6 chopped onions
- 15 ml (1 tbsp) fresh coriander, chopped
- 15 ml (1 tbsp) extra virgin olive oil
- Salt
- Ground black pepper

## DIRECTIONS

- Slice onion into rings.
- Brown onions in olive oil.
- Once onions are ready, add the Blanche de Chambly beer.
- Reduce, then add the cream and simmer a few minutes.
- Season with salt and pepper to taste.
- Garnish with coriander before serving.

*NOTE: Ideal for poultry.*

RECIPE AND PAIRINGS

RECIPE

BEER PAIRINGS

# HOT PEPPER SAUCE

## INGREDIENTS

*FOR 500 ML (2 CUPS)*

- 250 ml (1 cup) Blonde de Chambly or À Tout le Monde beer
- 340 g (3/4 lb) Jamaican hot peppers and Madame Jeanette peppers, seeds removed and diced
- 1 French shallot, coarsely chopped
- Half a carrot, sliced
- 1 large garlic clove, sliced in half
- 125 (1/2 cup) ml wine vinegar
- 10 ml (2 tsp) sea salt

## DIRECTIONS

- Place peppers, French shallots, half-carrot and garlic in a medium-size saucepan.
- Bring to a boil and simmer at medium-low heat for about 15 minutes until vegetables are tender. Let sit until warm.
- With a mixer, mix all the ingredients until homogeneous. Pour through a sieve.

*NOTE: The hot pepper sauce can be kept in the refrigerator for 2 to 3 weeks. It's the perfect addition to chicken or shrimp.*

# SAUCE FOR BEEF BOURGIGNON WITH LA FIN DU MONDE

## INGREDIENTS

*SERVES 4*

- 150 ml (5/8 cup) La Fin du Monde beer
- 2 fresh shallots
- Extra virgin olive oil
- 30 ml (2 tbsp) fresh coriander, chopped finely
- 1 egg yolk
- 100 ml (3/8 cup) vegetable broth
- 100 ml (3/8 cup) beef broth
- 15 ml (1 tbsp) all-purpose flour
- Salt and Madagascar black pepper

## DIRECTIONS

- In a salad bowl, beat the egg yolk in the broth (mix of vegetable and beef) and the beer, and add the shallots and the coriander.
- Add salt and pepper and thicken with a bain-marie, stirring constantly.
- Dissolve flour in a bit of water and add to the sauce to thicken.
- Continue cooking, stirring constantly, until the sauce is smooth.

**RECIPE**

**BEER PAIRINGS**

**RECIPE AND PAIRINGS**

MARINATED JALAPEÑOS WITH À TOUT LE MONDE

CARAMELIZED ONIONS WITH MAUDITE

# HOMEMADE MARMALADE WITH BLANCHE DE CHAMBLY

## INGREDIENTS

*FOR 6 JARS (8 OZ EACH)*

- 500 ml (2 cups) Blanche de Chambly beer
- 1.2 kg (2 lb) oranges, thoroughly washed and brushed
- 700 ml (3 cups) cane sugar
- 700 ml (3 cups) coarse sugar
- Juice from one lemon

## DIRECTIONS

- Peel the oranges (remove the white membrane as well). Cut the pulp into cubes.
- Slice the skin thinly and blanch three times.
- In a large pan, combine the skin, orange flesh, beer and the two kinds of sugar. Bring to a boil and simmer 1 hour on medium heat, stirring frequently, until the marmalade is translucent.
- Add the lemon juice and continue cooking for another minute.
- Pour into marmalade jars.

*The perfect gift for your mother-in-law!*

RECIPE

BEER PAIRINGS

*The perfect recipe to pimp your Sunday afternoon brunch!*

# CARAMELIZED ONIONS WITH MAUDITE

## INGREDIENTS

*FOR 500 ML (2 CUPS)*

- 350 ml (1 1/2 cups) Maudite beer
- 30 ml (2 tbsp) extra virgin olive oil
- 6 red onions, thinly sliced
- 1 garlic clove, sliced
- 15 ml (1 tbsp) brown sugar
- 15 ml (1 tbsp) maple syrup
- 30 ml (2 tbsp) white wine vinegar
- A pinch of salt
- Ground black pepper

## DIRECTIONS

- In a large pot, heat the garlic in the olive oil on medium heat.
- Add the onions and cook, stirring regularly, for about 10 minutes or until the onions soften.
- Add the brown sugar, maple syrup, vinegar, salt and pepper.
- Cook for a few minutes, stirring constantly.
- Add the beer and bring to a boil.
- Reduce heat to medium and simmer, uncovered. Stir from time to time for about 30 minutes or until liquid is completely evaporated and onions are golden.
- Let cool.

*NOTE: Sprinkle with finely chopped parsley before serving for a beautiful presentation.*

RECIPE

BEER PAIRINGS

# MARINATED JALAPEÑOS WITH À TOUT LE MONDE

## INGREDIENTS

*FOR 350 ML (1 1/2 CUPS)*

- 250 ml (1 cup) À Tout le Monde or Blonde de Chambly beer
- 30 ml (2 tbsp) cane sugar
- 15 ml (1 tbsp) salt
- 125 ml (1/2 cup) white vinegar
- 5 large Jalapeños peppers, finely sliced

## DIRECTIONS

- In a saucepan, mix sugar, salt and vinegar. Cook on medium-high heat while stirring until the salt and sugar are dissolved and remove from heat.
- Add the beer and pour in a preserves jar.
- Refrigerate for about 20 minutes.
- Add the peppers in the jar and close tightly.
- Refrigerate for at least 24 hours.
- Serve on nachos, in a burger or any other tasty dish to add some kick.

# RHUBARB JAM WITH ÉPHÉMÈRE APPLE

## INGREDIENTS

*FOR 1 LARGE JAR*

- 150 ml (2/3 cup) Éphémère Apple or Blanche de Chambly beer
- 200 g (1/2 lbs) rhubarb
- 200 g (1/2 lbs) McIntosh apple
- 250 ml (1 cup) cane sugar
- 250 ml (1 cup) crystal sugar
- 5 ml (1 tsp) powdered cinnamon
- 5 ml (1 tsp) nutmeg
- Juice from half a lemon

## DIRECTIONS

- Slice the peeled apple thinly and soak in the beer for about 1 hour.
- Peel the rhubarb and cut into cubes.
- Combine the fruit, lemon juice, sugars, cinnamon, nutmeg and the beer in a bowl.
- Cover and macerate at room temperature for about 12 hours.
- Separate the fruit from the syrup and sift.
- Bring syrup to a boil in a pan and simmer for a few minutes.
- Incorporate the macerated fruit and simmer for 5 to 10 minutes.
- Pour into a jar. Impress your guests at your next family brunch.

# FOOD TRUCK DISHES

## – Snacking... on the road –

The Unibroue "Bières et Bouffe" food truck travelled across the country last summer in search of fans. Food lovers had the chance to see our food truck and savor delicious recipes at various festivals and gatherings. Our experts mastered the art of combining beer and dishes and are happy to share their discoveries! Recreate these winning recipes in the comfort of your home.

LA FIN DU MONDE

UNIBROUE

ASIAN BUNS

# PORK FLANK BRAISED WITH BEER

### INGREDIENTS

- 2 bottles La Fin du Monde (34lml / 12 oz)
- 750 g (1.5 lb) pork flank, smoked with the rind
- 500 ml (2 cups) water or veal stock to enhance flavours
- 1 carrot
- 15 ml (1 tbsp) powdered lemongrass
- 15 ml (1 tbsp) sesame oil
- 2 celery stalks
- 2 bay leaves
- 2 sprigs of thyme
- 4 garlic cloves, crushed
- 30 ml (2 tbsp) brown sugar

**RECIPE**

**BEER PAIRINGS**

### DIRECTIONS

- Season the pork flank with salt, pepper and powdered lemongrass and sear on each side in the salted butter.
- Mix all the ingredients in an oven-safe container and heat at 300°F or in a crockpot for 8 hours.
- When cooked, remove from the juice and let sit.
- Sear the pork flank again in the sesame oil to give it a nice colour.

## SAUCE

### INGREDIENTS

- 200 g (1/2 cup) beer mayonnaise*
- 25 g (2 tsp) light soya
- A pinch of black sesame seeds

## BUNS

### INGREDIENTS

- 4 store-bought Asian buns
- Carrot, julienned
- Napa cabbage, julienned
- 15 ml (1 tbsp) rice vinegar
- Lime juice
- Fresh coriander
- 15 ml (1 tbsp) olive oil

### DIRECTIONS

- Cut carrot and Napa cabbage into juliennes (season with a bit of rice vinegar, lime juice and salt).
- Add a bit of fresh coriander.
- Heat the buns with steam or toast in olive oil to taste.

*See p.45 for the beer mayonnaise recipe.

*Tasty homemade steamed buns, just like in the restaurant!*

## TARTARE

### INGREDIENTS

- 500 g (I lb) organic salmon without the skin, cut into small dice
- 20 g (I oz) French shallots or green shallots, chopped finely
- 20 g (I oz) coriander, chopped finely
- I0 g (I/2 oz) capers, chopped finely
- 40 ml (I/8 cup) extra virgin olive oil
- 20 ml (4 tsp) seasoned rice vinegar
- I0 drops of green spicy sauce
- Juice of half an orange
- A pinch of sea salt and ground pepper to taste

### DIRECTIONS

- Mix all the ingredients and serve cold.
- Garnish with cranberry compote, orange zest, fresh coriander and coloured tortilla chips.

## CRANBERRY COMPOTE

### INGREDIENTS

- One half-bottle of Blanche de Chambly beer (34Iml / I2 oz)
- 500 ml (2 cups) dried cranberry
- 200 ml (3/4 cup) white sugar
- Half a cinnamon stick to taste

### DIRECTIONS

Mix all the ingredients in a small saucepan and simmer at medium heat until you obtain a compote texture (about I5 minutes).

*The fancy meal for health nuts!*

RECIPE

BEER PAIRINGS

# SALMON TARTARE

# BRAISED BEEF SANDWICH

*THIS RECIPE SERVES 8*

## INGREDIENTS

- 2 bottles of Maudite beer (341 ml / 12 oz)
- 1 kg (2.2 lb) beef scoter, cut into two pieces
- 2 red onions, coarsely chopped
- 2 large carrots, coarsely chopped
- 4 celery stalks, coarsely chopped
- 5 bay leaves
- 4 crushed garlic cloves with the skin
- 2 Jalapeños peppers with seeds, cut in half
- 200 ml (3/4 cup) honey
- 500 ml (2 cups) veal stock
- 8 hamburger or ciabatta buns
- Sauted mushrooms and onions
- Strong cheddar slices
- Beer mayonnaise*
- Chopped lettuce

## DIRECTIONS

- Season the scoter with salt, pepper and powdered cumin and sear all sides in salted butter.
- Mix all the ingredients in an oven-safe container and heat at 300°F or cook in a slow-cooker for 8 hours.
- Remove the meat from the heat and pull it while still hot.
- Garnish the burger or ciabatta bun with beef, sauted mushrooms and onions, a slice of strong cheddar, beer mayonnaise and the chopped lettuce.
- Use the cooking juices to dip your sandwich.

*Beer mayonnaise recipe, page 45.*

### RECIPE

### BEER PAIRINGS

## INGREDIENTS

- 1 package of rice vermicelli, cooked and drained
- Carrot, cut into juliennes
- Celery, cut into juliennes
- Napa cabbage, chopped
- Unsalted peanuts
- Fresh coriander
- Thai peppers
- Salt and pepper
- 15 ml (1 tbsp) black sesame seeds

### Shrimp marinade

- Half a bottle of La Fin du Monde beer (34lml / 12 oz)
- 500 ml (2 cups) peeled shrimp
- 150 ml (5/8 cup) seasoned rice vinegar
- 100 ml (3/8 cup) extra virgin olive oil
- 50 ml (3 tbsp) fish sauce
- 50 ml (3 tbsp) white sugar
- A pinch of salt and ground pepper

## DIRECTIONS

- Mix all the ingredients for the marinade and marinate the shrimp for at least 24 hours.
- Drain the shrimp and sauté them at medium-high in extra virgin olive oil. Season with salt, pepper and black sesame seeds.
- Serve on rice vermicelli, julienned carrot, julienned celery, Napa cabbage, unsalted peanuts, fresh coriander and chopped Thai peppers to taste. Add vinaigrette to taste.

# VINAIGRETTE BASE

## INGREDIENTS

- 75 ml (1/3 cup) La Fin du Monde beer
- 75 ml (1/3 cup) seasoned rice vinegar
- 75 ml (1/3 cup) fish sauce
- 75 ml (1/3 cup) sesame oil and extra virgin olive oil

*The perfect summer lunch for a sunny Sunday afternoon on a terrace.*

RECIPE

BEER PAIRINGS

# SHRIMP VERMICELLI

*THIS RECIPE SERVES 2*

## INGREDIENTS

- I bottle of À Tout le Monde beer
  (34lml / 12 oz bottle)
- 500 g (1,1 lbs) of boneless,
  skinless chicken thighs
- I L (34 fl oz) of mango puree
- 250 ml (1 cup) of seasoned rice vinegar
- 3 tbsp. of honey
- I bunch of mint or Thai basil
- Sea salt and pink peppercorns

## DIRECTIONS

- Skewer the chicken
- Run the other ingredients through a food
  processor until you get a smooth consistency.
  Marinate the chicken in the mixture for at
  least 24 hours.
- Grill the chicken on the BBQ, making sure
  to reserve half the marinade for a side sauce.
- This is a street food recipe; the ingredients
  can be adjusted to taste.
- Alternative: This recipe can also be made with
  beef filets or chicken breasts, but the results
  will be dryer than the chicken thighs.

RECIPE

BEER PAIRINGS

# CHICKEN SATAY WITH MANGO AND PINK PEPPERCORNS

# SPARE RIBS WITH MAUDITE

*THIS RECIPE SERVES 4*

## INGREDIENTS

- 2 bottles of Maudite beer
  (34lml / I2 oz bottles)
- 3.6 kg (8 lb) pork spare ribs
- 30 ml (2 tbsp) butter
- I Spanish onion, coarsely chopped
- I celery stalk, diced
- 2 leeks, sliced
- 2 carrots, sliced
- I tomato, chopped
- I litre veal stock
- 6 garlic cloves, chopped
- 3 Jalapeño peppers with the seeds
- 5 bay leaves
- 5 cloves
- Maudite BBQ sauce*
- Salt and ground pepper

*For the Maudite BBQ sauce recipe,
 turn to p.14

## DIRECTIONS

- Generously season spare ribs with salt
  and pepper.
- Sear the meat in a large, deep pan until
  you get a nice coloration. Set aside.
- In the same pan, sauté the mirepoix (onion,
  celery, leek, carrots, peppers, tomato) and
  garlic in butter, until the vegetables soften
  and get a nice coloration.
- Place the mirepoix, bay leaves and cloves
  in a large oven-safe dish. Place meat over
  the mirepoix and add the veal stock.
- Deglaze with the two beers and reduce by
  a quarter.
- Cover and macerate in the oven for 3 hours
  at 350°F. The humidity from the beer and
  vegetables will condensate to infuse the
  meat with the flavours coming from the
  mirepoix and the liquid.

- Remove from oven, turn the meat and
  continue cooking for another 2 hours.
- Remove the spare ribs from the sauce
  and drain.
- Cool, then grill on the BBQ, basting with
  the Maudite BBQ sauce and serve hot.

RECIPE

BEER PAIRINGS

# BREADING

## INGREDIENTS

- 250 ml (1 cup) Raftman or
  À Tout le Monde beer
- 185 ml (3/4 cup) flour
- 60 ml (1/4 cup) fine polenta
- 5 ml (1 tsp) Cajun spices
- 5 ml (1 tsp) paprika
- 5 ml (1 tsp) Cayenne
- 5 ml (1 tsp) ground mustard
- A pinch of salt and white pepper

## DIRECTIONS

- Mix the dry ingredients, add the beer
  and whip. For a light breading,
  add more beer.
- Cut large pickles into wedges or slices,
  drain well on brown paper and dip into
  the breading.
- Fry at 375°F for about 4 minutes or until
  pickles are golden. Place the fried pickles
  on brown paper to absorb the extra grease.
- Serve with a ranch sauce or a sour cream
  (500 ml (2 cups) of sour cream, 150 ml (5/8
  cup) beer, chopped chives, salt and pepper).

RECIPE

BEER PAIRINGS

# FRIED PICKLES
# WITH RAFTMAN

# PANACOTTA WITH ÉPHÉMÈRE BLUEBERRY

## MIXTURE

### INGREDIENTS

- 750 ml (3 cups) 15% whipping cream
- 150 ml (5/8 cup) white sugar
- Half a vanilla bean
- Gelatine – one package and a half
  (dissolve in water as instructed
  on the package)

### DIRECTIONS

- Lightly simmer the cream and sugar for about
  5 minutes with half a vanilla bean (scraped),
  and then add the gelatine. Whip the mixture
  and remove from heat.
- Pour the liquid in ramekins and garnish with
  the blueberry compote.

## BLUEBERRY COMPOTE

### INGREDIENTS

- Half a bottle of Éphémère Blueberry
  (341ml / 12 oz)
- 750 ml (3 cups) fresh blueberries
- 125 ml (1/2 cup) white sugar

### DIRECTIONS

- Place all the ingredients into a pan and simmer
  at low heat until the beer is reduced to half.
- Let cool and serve with the panacotta.

*NOTE: You can garnish with chocolate
shavings, cocoa and a fresh mint leaf.
The blueberry mixture can also be
placed in the food processor to obtain
a smoother texture.*

RECIPE

BEER PAIRINGS

# POOR MAN'S PUDDING WITH MAUDITE

*Tastes like your grandmother's baking — but revisited. Perfect for the sweet tooth in you!*

*THIS RECIPE SERVES 8 TO 10*

## INGREDIENTS

**Syrup**

- I bottles of Maudite beer (34lml / 12 oz)
- 500 ml (2 cups) maple syrup
- 125 ml (I/2 cup) brown sugar

**Cake dough**

- 3 eggs
- 250 ml (I cup) sugar
- 250 ml (I cup) softened butter
- 250 ml (I cup) flour
- 15 ml (I tbsp) baking powder
- I ml (I/4 tsp) salt
- 125 ml (I/2 cup) milk
- 5 ml (I tsp) vanilla extract

## DIRECTIONS

- Preheat oven at 350 °F.
- Mix eggs, sugar and butter in the food processor or with an electric mixer. Set aside.
- In a bowl, combine flour, baking powder and salt. Set aside.
- In a small bowl, combine the milk and the vanilla. Alternately add the flour mixture and the milk mixture to the egg mixture. Blend for 2 to 3 minutes until the preparation is homogenous. Set aside.
- In a pan, bring the Maudite beer, the maple syrup and the brown sugar to a boil. Pour into a cake pan and cover with the cake dough.
- Bake for 35 to 45 minutes or until a toothpick comes out clean.

*NOTE: For more sauce, melt 150 g (3/4 lb) brown sugar, 150 g (1/3 lb) unsalted butter and add 1 Maudite beer (341ml / 12 oz). Bring to a boil. This sauce can be kept for a few minutes.*

### RECIPE AND PAIRING

MAUDITE

FOOD TRUCK DISHES

# ON THE ROAD

## – Festive times, tasty memories –

The Unibroue "Bières et Bouffe" Food truck is on the road... and is coming over
to spoil you in your own backyard. A contest was put together to bring our recipe creators
and beer experts over to a fan's house to create wonderful recipes. The following recipes
are perfect for small and large appetites and to savour with the ones you love.

PANKO CRABCAKE

## INGREDIENTS

- 2 bottles of Blanche de Chambly beer (341 ml / 12 oz)
- 454 g (1 lb) uncooked snow crab or cooked crab, crab meat, blue crab or canned crab
- 90 ml (3/8 cup) panko breading
- 100 ml (3/8 cup) flour
- 2 eggs
- Juice of half a lemon
- 105 ml (3/8 cup) mayonnaise
- 2 chopped chive strands
- 30 ml (2 tbsp) chopped coriander
- 30 ml (2 tbsp) chopped parsley
- Zest from one orange
- 2 ml smoked paprika
- 2 ml garlic powder
- One small pinch of cumin
- Salt and pepper to taste

### Broth for uncooked crab

- 1 carrot
- 1 celery stick
- Half an onion
- 1 garlic clove
- 1 bay leaf
- 15 ml (1 tbsp) chopped coriander
- Juice from one orange

# CRAB

## POACHED OPTION - FRESH

### DIRECTIONS

- In a pot, pour 2 Blanche de Chambly beers (keep 20 ml (4 tsp) for the spicy mayonnaise), 250 ml (1 cup) water, one diced carrot, one chopped celery stalk, half an onion (chopped), the garlic, one bay leaf, a bit of fresh coriander to taste and the orange juice.
- Bring to a boil and add the crab in the broth. Poach for 15 to 20 minutes at very low heat.
- Remove from heat and let cool.
- Remove the meat from the shell and go to the "recipe (continued)" section.

## ALREADY COOKED OPTION

### DIRECTIONS

- Remove meat from the shell and/or rinse if using canned crab.
- Place the crab meat in a food processor at low speed to chop into fine pieces.
- Place crab meat in a bowl.
- Pour the Blanche de Chambly on the crab and cover with plastic wrap.
- Macerate for 24 hours.

## RECIPE (CONTINUED)

- Drain the crab.
- In a bowl, combine the crab meat, 60 ml (1/4 cup) panko, one egg, 30 ml (2 tbsp) mayonnaise, juice from one lemon, salt, pepper, cumin, chopped parsley, coriander and chives.
- Shape into 4 patties and refrigerate for at least 45 minutes.

RECIPE

BEER PAIRINGS

# BREADING

### DIRECTIONS

- Place one egg, beaten, in a plate and the flour in another.
- Place 30 ml (2 tbsp) of panko breading and a third plate.
- Dip the patties in the flour, then in the egg and finally in the panko and brown in a pan or fry in the oven at 375°F until they are nicely golden. Place on a paper to drain.

# BEER MAYONNAISE

### DIRECTIONS

- Combine the rest of the mayonnaise, 20 ml (4 tsp) Blanche de Chambly, the zest from an orange, the smoked paprika, the garlic powder, the salt and pepper and blend in the food processor.
- Place a dollop of mayonnaise on each of the warm patties.
- Garnish with a wedge of citrus and fresh coriander.

# MODERN-DAY GRILLED CHEESE

*With a tomato and basil cream soup on the side, the flavours are enhanced.*

*THIS RECIPE SERVES 4*

# ONION CONFIT

### INGREDIENTS

- 250 ml (1 cup) Maudite beer
- 4 chopped onions
- 15 ml (1 tbsp) butter
- 15 ml (1 tbsp) balsamic vinegar
- 15 ml (1 tbsp) brown sugar

### DIRECTIONS

- Melt the butter at medium heat in a non-adhesive pan. Add the onions and brown.
- Deglaze the onions with the beer and reduce heat.
- Simmer until onions turn a caramel colour.
- Add the brown sugar and balsamic vinegar. Reduce for about 10 minutes.
- Let cool and refrigerate.

# GRILLED CHEESE

### INGREDIENTS

- 8 slices of home-style bread with nuts
- 250 g (1/2 lb) raclette cheese of your choice
- 1 Granny Smith apple
- 200 g (1/2 lb) bacon, non-sliced
- 60 ml (1/2 cup) butter

### DIRECTIONS

- Cut the apple into thin slices.
- Cut the bacon into thin slices and fry lightly without making it crispy. Set aside.
- Slice the nut bread in eight thick slices.
- Butter the slices on one side only.
- Grill on low heat on both sides.
- Enjoy.

RECIPE

BEER PAIRINGS

*THIS RECIPE SERVES 4*

## INGREDIENTS

- 125 ml (4 oz) Raftman or À Tout le Monde beer
- 1.5 litre cabbage (white, red or Napa) chopped finely in the food processor or with a knife
- 180 ml (2/3 cup) mayonnaise
- 30 ml (2 tbsp) white vinegar
- 30 ml (2 tbsp) sugar
- 1/4 of a bunch of chopped Italian parsley
- Salt and pepper

## DIRECTIONS

- In a large bowl, pour 60 ml of the Raftman beer on the cabbage. Mix and marinate for about an hour.
- In another container, combine the mayonnaise and the rest of the beer. Season and mix well.
- Combine all the ingredients.
- Season with salt to taste and generously with pepper.
- Refrigerate for at least an hour before serving for the flavours to blend properly.

RECIPE

BEER PAIRINGS

5 lbs cabbage
32 happy guests
1 memorable night
Do it again!

## COLESLAW
## WITH
## RAFTMAN

PULLED BEEF POUTINE

# PULLED BEEF

## INGREDIENTS

- I Trois Pistoles or Maudite beer (34lml / I2 oz)
- 800 g (I.5 lb) beef scoter
- 2 carrots, diced
- I garlic clove, finely chopped
- I onion, diced
- 2 celery stalks, diced
- 2 bay leaves
- One pinch of paprika
- Peppercorn
- I package of fresh curd cheese
- Fried onions
- Fresh parsley, chopped

## DIRECTIONS

- Sear the beef scoter, previously cut into 4 inch pieces, in a pan with butter and salt and pepper.
- Transfer the browned beef pieces in a deep/ creuset dish and cover with half water, half beer. The meat must be covered with liquid.
- Add the carrots, celery, onions, garlic, bay leaves, paprika and peppercorn.
- Cover and cook for I2 hours at 200°F.
- Remove the meat and shred it while still hot.

*NOTE: Pour the cooking juice through a sieve and let sit for 6 hours in the refrigerator. Then remove the grease and use the cooking juice in the gravy.*

# POUTINE GRAVY

## INGREDIENTS

- 200 ml (3/4 cup) Trois Pistoles or Maudite beer
- I5 ml (I tbsp) chives, chopped
- 2 garlic cloves, chopped
- 75 ml (I/4 cup) sugar
- 75 ml (I/4 cup) balsamic vinegar
- I5 ml (I tbsp) butter
- 300 ml (I I/4 cup) cooking juice from the beer
- 45 ml (3 tbsp) tomato paste
- I pinch of Cayenne pepper
- 2 cloves
- I5 ml (I tbsp) turmeric
- 2 bay leaves
- 45 ml (3 tbsp) corn starch
- 100 ml (3/8 cup) cold water
- Salt
- Pepper

## DIRECTIONS

- In a pan, at medium heat, combine the sugar, chives and garlic and let it melt until a caramel is obtained.
- Deglaze with the balsamic vinegar, add the butter and reduce to half.
- Add the cooking juice from the beef, the beer, the tomato paste and the spices. Simmer for about 5 minutes.
- Dilute the corn starch in cold water and whip the mix into the gravy. Season and serve.

# HOMEMADE FRIES

## INGREDIENTS

- Idaho or Yukon Gold potatoes
- Peanut or canola oil
- Salt

## DIRECTIONS

- Peel the potatoes, leaving a bit of the skin on and cut into I cm (I/2 inch) thick pieces. Let them sit in cold water for an hour, drain and pat dry.
- Pour the oil in a fryer or large pot and heat to 325°F. Blanch the fries for 2-3 minutes. Remove the fries from the oil and drain well.
- Heat the oil up to 375°F. Place the fries in the oil for another 4 or 5 minutes of cooking or until they are golden.
- Drain the fries and cover with a paper towel to remove excess oil.

# ASSEMBLY

## DIRECTIONS

- Place the golden fries in the serving dishes.
- Place the pulled beef on the fries.
- Add the delicious curd cheese.
- Pour a generous portion of poutine gravy to complete.

*NOTE: Garnish with fried onions or a bit of fresh parsley, finely chopped, for a very trendy gourmet look and a delight for the taste buds. Enjoy with a delicious Unibroue beer for an unforgettable experience.*

RECIPE AND PAIRINGS

# COOKING WITH UNIBROUE

## – Our chefs in your kitchen –

In order to create memorable culinary experiences in our fans' homes, our chefs took your recipes and revamped them using Unibroue products. In a comfortable setting, 3 lucky winners welcomed our team to help them create enhanced versions of their favorite recipes. At the end of the day, there were happy stomachs and new recipes to try!

## INGREDIENTS

- Half a bottle of Trois Pistoles beer (341ml / 12 oz)
- 200 g (1/2 lb) cod fillet
- 75 g (2.5 oz) fresh white mushrooms
- 50 g (1.5 oz) onion
- Half a bunch of flat-leaf parsley
- One garlic clove, chopped
- Extra virgin olive oil
- A few cherry tomatoes
- 10 ml (2 tsp) brown sugar
- Salt and pepper

*"The cod can be replaced with other kinds of fish for variation!"*

*— Magali*

## DIRECTIONS

- Wash the mushrooms and cut them in half (in four pieces if they are very big) and set aside.
- Peel and slice onion thinly. Chop the garlic.
- Chop the parsley finely and mix in with the onion. Add the garlic and set the mixture aside.
- In a non-adhesive pan, sear the cod (previously seasoned with salt and pepper) in the extra virgin olive oil. Remove from heat and set aside.
- In the same pan, add a dash of extra virgin olive oil and sauté the garlic, onion, parsley and mushrooms. Midway through cooking, deglaze with the beer and add the brown sugar. Bring to a boil, lower to medium heat and place the fish in the sauce. Cook for about 4 minutes depending on the fish thickness.
- Add the fresh parsley and a few cherry tomatoes cut into wedges to the sauce a few seconds before serving. Place the fish on the plate and cover with sauce.
- Season with salt and pepper (to taste).
- Serve with jasmine rice or homemade mashed potatoes with nutmeg.

**RECIPE**

**BEER PAIRINGS**

# COD FILLETS WITH TROIS PISTOLES

BY
MAGALI NAULIN

# BREAD WITH BEER AND GARLIC FLOWERS

### BY
### MANON GODIN

*"To get nice slices, turn the bread over before slicing."*

*— Manon*

## INGREDIENTS

- 375 ml (1 1/2 cup) Trois Pistoles beer
- 3 cups all-purpose flour
- 30 ml (2 tbsp) baking powder
- 45 ml (3 tbsp) golden brown sugar
- Softened butter
- 5 ml (1 tsp) salt
- 60 ml (1/4 cup) melted butter
- 3 garlic flower stems
- 3 candied garlic cloves
- 125 ml (1/2 cup) Gran Padano parmesan

## DIRECTIONS

- Preheat oven at 350 °F.
- Grease a bread pan with butter.
- Combine flour, baking powder, brown sugar, salt, beer and candied garlic. Place in the bread pan.
- Blend the garlic flower stems and the butter with a mixer.
- Place this mix on the bread dough with the parmesan and bake for 55 minutes.
- Let cool and turn out.

## SERVE WITH A BEER BUTTER

- 225 g (1/2 lb) softened butter
- 50 ml (3 tbsp) Blanche de Chambly beer
- 50 ml (3 tbsp) 35% cream

Blend in a food processor, place in a container and refrigerate for 12 hours.

RECIPE

BEER PAIRINGS

COOKING WITH UNIBROUE

# BACON JAM

### BY
### AMÉLIE TRÉPANIER

*THIS RECIPE SERVES 2*

## INGREDIENTS

- 375 ml (1 1/2 cup) La Fin du Monde beer
- 500 g (1 lb) smoked lard, diced
  (or use regular bacon with liquid smoke)
- 4 garlic cloves, chopped
- 1 chopped medium onion
- 45 ml (3 tbsp) brown sugar
- Tabasco sauce to taste
- 1 seedless Jalapeño pepper
- 250 ml (1 cup) coffee
- 60 ml (1/4 cup) apple cider vinegar
- 60 ml (1/4 cup) maple syrup
- Black pepper to taste
- 250 ml (1 cup) water
- A quarter of a bunch of oregano
- A pinch of pink pepper

## DIRECTIONS

- In a stew pot style saucepan,
  fry the lard in bunches until it is
  slightly golden and starts to get crispy.
  Cut into 1 inch pieces with scissors.
- Sauté the onion and garlic in the bacon
  grease on medium heat until they are
  translucent. Add the rest of the ingredients,
  except for the water, oregano and
  pink pepper.
- Simmer for about 2 hours, adding 60 ml
  (4 tbsp) of water every 25-30 minutes while
  stirring.
- Once it is ready, cool for about 15-20 minutes
  and pour into a food processor. Add the
  oregano and pink pepper. Start the food
  processor for 2-3 seconds to get a jam
  consistency or run longer for a smoother,
  pastier texture.

RECIPE

BEER PAIRINGS

**COOKING WITH UNIBROUE**

# PORK MEATBALLS

### BY
### JOSIANE PERRON

*"To welcome your guests in style, make sure they arrive when the stew's aroma fills the house."*

*— Josiane*

# MEATBALL MIXTURE

## INGREDIENTS

- 300 g (2/3 lb) ground pork
- I egg
- 40 ml bread crumbs
- 45 ml (3 tbsp) flour
- 15 ml (I tbsp) butter
- 60 ml (I/4 cup) dill bunch
- 60 ml (I/4 cup) flat-parsley bunch
- 2 ml (I/2 tsp) powdered mustard
- 10 ml (2 tsp) fresh ginger, grated
- One pinch of salt and ground pepper

## DIRECTIONS

- Mix all the ingredients. Make golf ball-size meatballs and cover with flour.
- Melt a knob of butter in a non-stick pan and sear the meatballs to obtain a nice coloration on the outside.
- Remove the meatballs and set aside.

# STEW

## INGREDIENTS

- 2 bottles of Noire de Chambly or Éphémère Apple beer (341 ml / 12 oz)
- 200 ml (7/8 cup) white mushrooms, sliced
- 10 ml (2 tsp) fresh garlic, chopped
- 60 ml (I/4 cup) onion, cut into small dice (brunoise)
- 150 ml (5/8 cup) chopped bacon
- 15 ml (I tbsp) butter
- 250 ml (I cup) maple syrup
- I litre water
- 350 ml (I I/2 cups) new potatoes, cut into wedges
- 100 ml (3/8 cup) carrots, diced
- 20 ml (4 tsp) white flour
- 20 ml (4 tsp) melted butter
- Fresh dill and parsley
- Salt and ground pepper

## DIRECTIONS

- Melt the butter in a saucepan and add the mushrooms, garlic, onion and bacon.
- Once it is nicely coloured, add the Noire de Chambly, the maple syrup and the water. Bring to a boil and add the meatballs. Reduce heat to medium-high and simmer for 15 minutes.
- Add the potatoes and the carrots. Cook for 15 minutes at medium-high heat and season with salt and fresh ground pepper.
- To finish, use a whip mix the flour with the melted butter and add to the gravy.
- Garnish with chopped fresh dill and parsley.

RECIPE

BEER PAIRINGS

# FAVORITES AND CLASSICS

## – Comfort in your plate –

Happiness is staying home and preparing comfort food! Here are our favorites to bring a smile to your face and to warm you up on those cold winter nights. It is said that dishes are even better when we associate them with happy memories. What are you waiting for to create them?

## INGREDIENTS

- 65 ml (1/4 cup) Don de Dieu beer
- 2 big vidalia onions, cut in half then finely sliced
- 65 ml (1/4 cup) butter
- Olive oil
- 175g (6 oz) pancetta, cut in small cubes
- 15 ml (1 tbsp) fresh thyme
- 500 ml (2 cups) Gruyère cheese, grated
- 500 ml (2 cups) cheddar cheese, grated
- 125 ml (1/2 cup) 5% sour cream
- 125 ml (1/2 cup) light cream cheese
- 1 scallion, finely sliced
- Salt and ground pepper

## DIRECTIONS

- Preheat oven at 200°C (400°F).
- In a big skillet at medium heat, melt the butter and add the onions. Add about 30 ml (2 tbsp) olive oil, season with salt and pepper then stir well. Cook slowly for 8-10 minutes while stirring often. Onions must not sear! Lower heat if that is the case.
- Meanwhile, in a skillet at medium heat, add a small drizzle of olive oil and cook the pancetta for 5-6 minutes until it gets crispy. Deglaze with the beer and scrape the bottom in order to grab all the flavours then pour in the onion mix. Add also the fresh thyme and stir well.
- Continue cooking the onions for about 10 minutes, stirring often, until they are dark and caramelized and the liquid is evaporated.
- Pour the onions in a big bowl and add the Gruyère cheese, 250 ml (1 cup) cheddar, sour cream and cream cheese. Stir well to combine and pour in a baking dish.
- Place in the oven and cook for 20 minutes. Remove from oven, stir well and add the rest of the cheddar on top. Place back in oven and cook at broil for 2-3 minutes until cheese is golden. Let cool 10 minutes. Garnish with scallions and serve with croutons, chips and veggies.

RECIPE

BEER PAIRINGS

# CHEEZY DIP WITH BEER CARAMELIZED ONIONS

# GRILLED BEEF BACK STEAK

## MARINATED WITH BLUEBERRIES AND BALSAMIC VINEGAR

*Perfect after a ski day, a bike ride, a soccer game...*

### INGREDIENTS

- 65 ml (1 tsp) Éphémère Blueberry or Elderberry beer
- 250 ml (1 cup) blueberries or elderberries
- 85 ml (1/3 cup) extra virgin olive oil
- 65 ml (1/4 cup) balsamic vinegar
- 15 ml (1 tbsp) honey
- 15 ml (1 tbsp) fresh thyme leaves
- 15 ml (1 tbsp) lemon juice
- Zest from half a lemon
- 1 kg (2.2 lb) back steak
- Salt and ground pepper

### DIRECTIONS

- Place all the ingredients, except for the meat, in a food processor and purée.
- Place the beef back steak in an air-tight container and pour the marinade on top.
- Cover, mix well and refrigerate for 6 to 24 hours. Stir occasionally.
- Remove from the refrigerator 30 minutes before grilling.
- Heat the barbecue to 200°C (400°F) (or a cast-iron ridged pan at medium-high heat) and lightly oil the surface.
- Place the meat on the grill and cook for 2-3 minutes. Rotate at 45° and continue cooking for 2-3 minutes. Turn the meat and repeat. Cooking 2-3 minutes, 45° rotation and cooking for 2-3 minutes. The meat should then be rare. Check the meat and continue cooking until you obtain the desired doneness.
- Remove from heat and place on a plate. Wrap with aluminum foil and let sit for 5 minutes.
- Cut into medallions and sprinkle with fleur de sel.

**RECIPE**

**BEER PAIRINGS**

## INGREDIENTS

- 200 ml (7/8 cup) Blanche de Chambly beer
- Store-bought pizza crust
- 1 large boneless, skinless chicken breast
- 30 ml (2 tbsp) vegetable oil
- 15 ml (1 tbsp) lemon pepper (or black pepper)
- 5 ml (1 tsp) garlic powder
- 5 ml (1 tsp) dried oregano
- 5 ml (1 tsp) dried basil
- 10 ml (2 tsp) salt
- 125 ml (1/2 cup) finely chopped fresh parsley
- 4 garlic cloves, crushed
- 30 ml (2 tbsp) extra virgin olive oil
- 15 ml (1 tbsp) garlic salt
- 7.5 ml herbes de Provence
- 1 onion, coarsely chopped
- 400 g (14 oz) grated strong cheddar
- 250 ml (1 cup) 35% country-style cream

## DIRECTIONS

- Cut the chicken into 2 cm cubes.
- Place chicken in a large bowl and pour in 200 ml Blanche de Chambly beer. Cover and refrigerate for 2 hours.
- Heat oil in a skillet. Drain chicken and sear over high heat with lemon pepper, garlic powder, basil, and 5 ml (1 tsp) of salt. Do not cook fully (no more than about 2 minutes per side). Set aside.
- Combine parsley, garlic, 5 ml (1 tsp) salt, 15 ml (1 tbsp) olive oil and freshly ground pepper in a small bowl using a fork. Set aside.
- Place pizza crust on a greased baking sheet.
- Preheat oven to 375°F.
- Drizzle a little olive oil over crust, then sprinkle evenly with garlic salt and herbes de Provence.
- Add an even layer of onions and chicken, then top with grated cheese.
- Sprinkle parsley and garlic mixture evenly over cheese.
- Top with 35% cream, making sure to cover entire pizza.
- Bake for 25 minutes. Finish under broiler for a few minutes to get a nice golden color. Let cool a few minutes before serving.

**RECIPE**

**BEER PAIRINGS**

# RUSTIC PIZZA WITH MARINATED CHICKEN

## IN BLANCHE DE CHAMBLY

# CHEESE FONDUE WITH BLONDE DE CHAMBLY

*Fondue + a few friends + a cozy fire + Blonde de Chambly beer = an unforgettable evening*

*THIS RECIPE SERVES 4*

### INGREDIENTS

- I bottle of Blonde de Chambly or
  À Tout le Monde beer (34I ml / I2 oz)
- 60 ml (I/4 cup) butter
- 60 ml (I/4 cup) flour
- 5 ml (I tsp) powdered mustard
- I0 ml (2 tsp) Worcestershire sauce
- II0 g (I/2 cup) grated old cheddar
- II0 g (I/2 cup) grated Jarlsberg
- II0 g (I/2 cup) grated cave-aged emmental
  (or cave-aged gruyère)
- I garlic clove
- Pepper to taste

### DIRECTIONS

- In a large pot, melt the butter.
- Incorporate the flour slowly with a whip
  to make a roux.
- Gradually add the beer, whipping continuously
  to avoid lumps. The mixture should thicken.
- Add the mustard and Worcestershire sauce.
- Still whipping, add the cheese in three
  portions, making sure it is melted before
  adding the next portion.
- Season with pepper, to taste.
- Cut the garlic clove in half and rub it inside
  thefondue pot. Add the garlic clove to the
  cheese fondue mix.
- Pour the fondue in the pot and serve with
  baguette cubes, sausage pieces (of your
  choice) and small boiled potatoes.

**RECIPE**

**BEER PAIRINGS**

## INGREDIENTS

- 750 ml (3 cups) Don de Dieu beer
- 750 ml (3 cups) white navy beans, uncooked
- 65 ml (1/4 cup) maple syrup
- 15 ml (1 tbsp) salt
- Approximately 1.5 to 2L of water
- 1.2 kg (2.5 lb) picnic pork shoulder with the rind removed, cut into large cubes
- 30 ml (2 tbsp) duck fat (or olive oil)
- 2 large Spanish onions, finely chopped
- 3 celery stalks, sliced
- 3 large carrots, peeled, cut in half lengthwise and sliced
- 6 garlic cloves, finely chopped
- Olive oil
- 350g (3/4 lb) smoked bacon, cut into large cubes
- 30 ml (2 tbsp) tomato paste
- 250 ml (1 cup) white wine
- 750 ml (3 cups) chicken broth
- 1 bouquet garni (8 sprigs of chives, 5 sprigs of thyme, 3 bay leaves, 1 sprig of sage with 5-6 leaves, all stringed together)
- 1 can diced Italian tomatoes (796 ml / 27 oz)
- 4 confit duck legs
- 5 large pork and garlic sausages
- A handful of fresh parsley, chopped
- Salt and ground pepper

## DIRECTIONS

- In a large pot, combine the beans, beer, maple syrup, salt and enough water to cover up to 2 inches above the mixture. Mix and cover. Let soak for 12 hours. Bring to a boil, reduce heat and simmer for 45 minutes. Pour into a strainer, drain and set aside.
- In a large oven-safe saucepan (enameled cast-iron) at medium-high heat, add the duck fat and let it melt. Brown the pork cubes on all sides, a small quantity at a time, for 5-6 minutes until nicely colored. Season with salt and pepper. Transfert to a bowl and set aside.
- In the same saucepan, add the onion, celery, carrots and garlic followed by a drizzle of olive oil. Season with salt and pepper, mix well and sauté vegetables for 8 minutes to caramelize the vegetables. Add more oil if necessary.
- Add the bacon and tomato paste and mix well. Continue cooking for 2-3 minutes while stirring. Add the white wine and scrape the bottom and sides to release all the flavours.
- Add the chicken broth, bouquet garni and Italian tomatoes and bring to a boil. Reduce to low heat and simmer lightly for 30 minutes. Remove the bouquet garni and set aside.
- Preheat oven at 400°F. Place 2 duck confit legs on a large cooking sheet and heat for 10-12 minutes or until the skin is crispy. Remove from the oven, shred the meat and set aside.

- In a large frying pan, at medium heat, add a drizzle of olive oil and brown the sausage on both sides for about 10 minutes in total. Brown only, as the cooking will continue in the oven. Slice 2 of the sausages into large pieces. Do not cut the other sausages. Set aside.
- Place half the cooked beans in a large saucepan and mix well. Spread the shredded duck meat followed by the sausage pieces and cover with the rest of the beans. Spread evenly by lightly pressing down. Place the whole duck legs and the sausage on top and cook in the oven without covering for an hour and a half. Let stand for 5-10 minutes and garnish with fresh parsley before serving.

RECIPE

BEER PAIRINGS

# TYPICAL TOULOUSE CASSOULET

ÉPHÉMÈRE
APPLE PIE

## INGREDIENTS

- 250 ml (1 cup) Éphémère Apple beer
- 1 store-bought pie crust
- 15 ml (1 tbsp) butter
- 125 ml (1/2 cup) boiling water
- 60 ml (1/4 cup) corn starch
- 60 ml (1/4 cup) cold water
- 6 peeled apples

## DIRECTIONS

- In a saucepan, bring the water, Éphémère Apple beer and butter to a boil. Boil for 2 minutes.
- In a small bowl, dissolve the corn starch in cold water. Add to the boiling mixture to thicken.
- Place the apple pieces at the bottom of the pie crust and pour the mixture over them.
- Bake at 350°F for 30 to 45 minutes.

*NOTE: You can use 6 to 8 apples, depending on their size.*

*According to your preference, you can add whipped cream, a dollop of English cream or maple syrup to the pie slices.*

**RECIPE AND PAIRING**

## INGREDIENTS

- 250 ml (I cup) I7ᵉ Grande Réserve or Terrible or La Résolution beer (room temperature)
- 235 g (8 oz) 70% Dark Chocolate, chopped
- 190 ml (3/4 cup) caramel / toffee bits
- 90 ml (6 tbsp) melted butter
- 250 ml (I cup) unbleached flour
- 190 ml (3/4 cup) unsweetened cocoa powder
- 5 ml (I tsp) instant coffee
- I generous pinch of salt
- 4 large eggs (room temperature)
- 250 ml (I cup) white sugar
- 65 ml (1/4 cup) pecan nuts, coarsely chopped
- I cup semi-sweet chocolate chips
- Fleur de sel

## DIRECTIONS

- Preheat the oven to 375°
- Melt the chocolate, the caramel and the butter in a bain-marie. Mix well. Keep warm.
- In the meantime, pour the flour, cocoa, coffee and the salt in a big bowl and mix well. Set aside.
- Mix the eggs and sugar at high speed with an electric mixer for about 2-3 minutes, until you get a light and foamy texture.
- Pour the chocolate mixture into the egg mixture and mix at medium speed until homogenous. Then, add the flour mixture, the beer and nuts and continue to mix until homogenous.
- Cover a 9" x 13" edged baking pan with parchment paper. Pour in the mixture and sprinkle it with chocolate chips. Add fleur de sel to your liking.
- Oven bake for 25-30 minutes or until a toothpick inserted in the center comes out clean.

RECIPE AND PAIRINGS

GRANDE RÉSERVE 17 2016 · TERRIBLE · LA RÉSOLUTION

# CHOCOLATE CARAMEL BROWNIES

## À LA 17ᴱ GRANDE RÉSERVE

# INDEX

## BY BEER

## RECIPES AND PAIRINGS

### BLANCHE DE CHAMBLY

Beer and lime marinade for shrimp and fish ............ 11
Creamy Blanche de Chambly sauce ............ 16
Homemade marmalade with Blanche de Chambly ............ 19
Rhubarb jams with Éphémère Apple ............ 21
Salmon tartare ............ 26
Panacotta with Éphémère Blueberry ............ 39
Panko crabcake ............ 45
Coleslaw with Raftman ............ 48
Cheezy dip with beer caramelized onions ............ 66
Rustic pizza with marinated chicken ............ 70

### BLONDE DE CHAMBLY

Beer marinade and herb butter for pork tenderloin ............ 12
Hot pepper sauce ............ 17
Marinated Jalapeños with À Tout le Monde ............ 21
Shrimp vermicelli ............ 30
Chicken satay with mango and pink peppercorns ............ 32
Cheese fondue with Blonde de Chambly ............ 73

### NOIRE DE CHAMBLY

Steak sauce with Noire de Chambly ............ 16
Braised beef sandwich ............ 29
Panko crabcake ............ 45
Cod fillets with Trois Pistoles ............ 54
Pork meatballs ............ 61

### ÉPHÉMÈRE APPLE

Marinade for spicy chicken drumsticks ............ 13
Creamy Blanche de Chambly sauce ............ 16
Caramelized onions with Maudite ............ 20
Rhubarb jams with Éphémère Apple ............ 21
Asian buns ............ 25
Chicken satay with mango and pink peppercorns ............ 32
Modern-day grilled cheese ............ 47
Bread with beer and garlic flowers ............ 57
Bacon jam ............ 59
Typical Toulouse cassoulet ............ 74
Éphémère apple pie ............ 77

## ÉPHÉMÈRE BLUEBERRY
Panacotta with Éphémère Blueberry.................................39
Bread with beer and garlic flowers................................57
Grilled beef back steak.................................................69

## ÉPHÉMÈRE ELDERBERRY
Grilled beef back steak.................................................69

## À TOUT LE MONDE
Beer marinade and herb butter for pork tenderloin.............12
Hot pepper sauce.......................................................17
Marinated Jalapeños with À Tout le Monde.......................21
Chicken satay with mango and pink peppercorns...............32
Fried pickles with Raftman.............................................36
Coleslaw with Raftman..................................................48
Cheese fondue with Blonde de Chambly..........................73

## DON DE DIEU
Homemade marmalade with Blanche de Chambly...............19
Fried pickles with Raftman.............................................36
Cheezy dip with beer caramelized onions........................66
Rustic pizza with marinated chicken................................70
Typical Toulouse cassoulet............................................74

## RAFTMAN
Marinade for spicy chicken drumsticks.............................13
BBQ sauce with Maudite................................................14
Fried pickles with Raftman.............................................36
Coleslaw with Raftman..................................................48

## MAUDITE
Beer and lime marinade for shrimp and fish.......................11
BBQ sauce with Maudite................................................14
Caramelized onions with Maudite....................................20
Braised beef sandwich..................................................29
Spare ribs with Maudite.................................................35
Poor man's pudding with Maudite....................................41
Modern-day grilled cheese.............................................47
Pulled beef poutine......................................................51
Cheese fondue with Blonde de Chambly..........................73

## LA FIN DU MONDE
Sauce for beef bourguignon with La Fin du Monde..............17
Asian buns................................................................25
Salmon tartare............................................................26
Shrimp vermicelli.........................................................30
Bread with beer and garlic flowers................................57
Bacon jam.................................................................59
Pork meatballs............................................................61
Cheezy dip with beer caramelized onions........................66

## TROIS PISTOLES
Marinade for skirt steak.................................................13
Steak sauce with Noire de Chambly................................16
Sauce for beef bourguignon with La Fin du Monde..............17
Spare ribs with Maudite.................................................35
Pulled beef poutine......................................................51
Cod fillets with Trois Pistoles.........................................54
Bread with beer and garlic flowers................................57
Grilled beef back steak.................................................69

## 17ᴱ GRANDE RÉSERVE
Chocolate Caramel Brownies à la 17ᵉ Grande Réserve........78

## TERRIBLE
Marinade for skirt steak.................................................13
Chocolate Caramel Brownies à la 17ᵉ Grande Réserve........78

## LA RÉSOLUTION
Chocolate Caramel Brownies à la 17ᵉ Grande Réserve........78

GRAPHIC DESIGN • DOMINIQUE FIGEYS AND KARINE CÔTÉ
ARTISTIC GUIDANCE AND CULINARY DESIGN • STRETCH MRK
PHOTOS • JUK PHOTOGRAPHER
CULINARY GUIDANCE • 3GO L'AGENCE
RECIPE CREATION • LE LUNCHBOX COMPTOIR – CHEF PASCAL
TRANSLATION • LYNE BROCHU

A UNIBROUE PRODUCTION

# UNIBROUE

## SPECIAL CREDITS

COD FILLETS WITH BEER • ORIGINAL RECIPE BY MAGALI NAULIN
BREAD WITH BEER AND GARLIC FLOWERS • ORIGINAL RECIPE BY MANON GODIN
BACON JAM • ORIGINAL RECIPE BY AMÉLIE TRÉPANIER
PORK MEATBALLS • ORIGINAL RECIPE BY JOSIANE PERRON
THESE FOUR RECIPES WERE REVAMPED BY LE LUNCHBOX COMPTOIR – CHEF PASCAL

CHICKEN SATAY WITH MANGO AND PINK PEPPERCORNS • PASCAL BISSON
CHEEZY DIP WITH BEER CARAMELIZED ONIONS • SAMUEL JOUBERT
GRILLED BEEF BACK STEAK • SAMUEL JOUBERT
RUSTIC PIZZA WITH MARINATED CHICKEN • SAMUEL JOUBERT
TYPICAL TOULOUSE CASSOULET • SAMUEL JOUBERT
CHEESE FONDUE WITH BLONDE DE CHAMBLY • KATIA BURELLE
CHOCOLATE CARAMEL BROWNIES À LA 17ᴱ GRANDE RÉSERVE • SAMUEL JOUBERT